A TOXIC

MOTHER

A TOXIC MOTHER

How To Recognize One and Getting Out From Under

Alex Farrell

www.blkdogpublishing.com

CONTENTS

AUTHOR'S NOTE AND DISCLAIMER

This book was originally written as an act of catharsis for me, when things got particularly bad and it grew until it became this short book. It was written over some years and has sat on my laptop for some more, but reading it through again today, nothing changed and nothing has changed, even though my mother has been dead a while. History has a way of healing over, as Terry Pratchett had it, and I have now heard the sizzle of time mending itself as it races past me but although the past is indeed a different country, all of those who lived there and got out to tell the tale *must* tell the tale. For a lot of my life, I was lonely, scared and felt worthless. I was lucky and found enough people who disagreed with my assessment to persuade me that I was actually important enough – to them at least – to carry on. So, here is my story. It won't be your story, but if you can take just one nugget away – and hopefully have a laugh as well, because keeping a sense of humour is key – then my work here is, if not done, then at least begun.

Few names are used in this book but any that are are not those of the actual person. Events and the people involved have been changed for narrative purposes, to save embarrassment to those drawn in to my mother's orbit.

I also need to say that I have no qualifications whatsoever in mental health – these chapter headings are taken from a variety of 'test yourself' websites and the advice given is just a bit of common sense, with love from me to you.

INTRODUCTION TO THE INTRODUCTION

Since I began this book some time has passed, full of many lovely things which made this catharsis less at the forefront of my mind. So, since that beginning and in the last few weeks, my mother has died. She lasted for an almost unprecedented fifteen days on end of life pathway, showing that even in dying she could cause problems. Family feuds have erupted everywhere, mostly fuelled by the fact that few people outside me and my very immediate family (husband and to a lesser extent children) had any idea of what it has been like living my whole life under the dark umbrella of her barely veiled hatred and derision. The content of the book that I will be writing to bring it to completion after this event won't change – unlike some people, for me she has not become a dear saintly little old lady, just because she has finally died.

Alex Farrell

INTRODUCTION

'Toxic parents' are all over the internet, how to decide whether you have one, what to do about it and so on. The bottom line is, if you have one, you don't need to look up a website to check on it. You will just *know*. The lightbulb moment can come at any time – I think mine was when I was still at infants' school, but I was a bit of a precocious kid – but when it *does* come, you'll look back and click your metaphorical fingers and say 'Of *course!*' Toxic parents are not just parents (usually just one, fortunately, and usually, sadly, a mother) who are strict, who have very strong rules around the house etc. In fact, parents who know their place and yours in the world are anything but toxic as a rule. They don't invade your space, and by space, I mean life; they give you room to grow, just gently herding you back if you stray too far. When you are too big to herd, they wait there with a big safety net to catch you before you fall too far. No, toxic parents are essentially a cancer in your world and finding them, cutting them out (which doesn't necessarily mean cutting off all contact, see later) and healing has to be done as soon as possible.

Sadly, my 'cancer' has been with me all my life and despite my not loving or even liking my mother and knowing for sure she feels the same, I have always done my best to make sure she is as happy as she can be – which I suspect isn't much – and making sure, back in the day when these people were alive, that she didn't take out her bottomless spite on my very beloved grandparents, my stepdad (hereinafter called my dad because after all, a dad is who brings you up, in a best case scenario) and my brother. It's too late now to test, because she has dementia, but I would guess that she has always suffered from a slew of mental issues, narcissism being just one.

However, just recently, she stepped over the line, the line that I had drawn so far down the road I thought it would never be reached. I won't go into detail here, because others are involved, but let's just say it was an act of disrespect, jealousy and vitriol that just made me say 'Enough!' When I stopped shaking, having my first and (please, Universe, let it be so) last panic attack in a supermarket, I decided that this was it. I would be civil, I would speak if spoken to, but beyond that, nothing.

Fortunately, I have a wonderful family (I'm talking strictly non-extended here) and better friends than my mother would say I deserve, and they have backed me to the hilt. My husband has known me as near to all my life as makes no difference and he has been waiting for this day practically since the day we became a couple – it's been a long haul and for that, I apologise. Make sure, anyone reading this, that you don't throw the baby out with the bathwater. Your nearest and dearest matter more than the non-appeasable monster who gave birth to you – trust me, they do.

After a near-death experience in my tiny family some years ago, I had some therapy to get rid of some aftereffects and my lovely therapist said if you can't hold your friends in your hands – in other words, you have more friends than fingers – then you have too many. And that, in my case at least, is very true. In fact, when I count them up, my thumbs are spare and I feel happy that way. They have been the most amazing resource of love and care and I really recommend that you embrace your friends and let them know what you're going through. Not by whingeing about what she said and what you said all the time – because that can be a bit wearing

– but a short email if you don't feel up to talking about it, explaining the situation. You will find that they are right behind you and they will understand. Because the bottom line is that they don't see the failed, ugly, fat loser that you have been told you are – they see you. And they love what they see.

If you do check online to see what constitutes a toxic parent, you will find lists of various length and they all say 'if you tick so and so many, then that's what you have'. You won't be surprised to find you have a toxic parent, but you may be surprised by how many you tick. I tried practically every one out there and however many categories there were, I could tick them all. But you may find that there are one or two areas where your parent doesn't fit the pattern, perhaps because of a strong family member reining them in just a little.

It was hard for me to begin this book and harder still to know how to proceed beyond the introduction. I have started to read many 'misery memoirs' in my time and have always given up before halfway because they are all a bit the same. Once you have established that the writer's mother/father/carer locked them in the coal cellar routinely, it doesn't really change much from thereon in. And of course, there are stories all the time in the press and online about children and young adults who have been imprisoned for years in cellars and attics all around the world. This is appalling and your heart has to go out to them, but there are people imprisoned by their parents who are walking around the world, apparently free. But they aren't. Their bonds are as unbreakable as any chain – or at least, so they seem.

I am not an expert in any form of therapy or anything else. But I have lived with a toxic parent for the best part of seven decades, so I suppose I know whereof I speak if anyone does. Thinking about how to shape this book and to avoid the interminable she said, she did stuff, I decided to make each of the usual points in 'have you got a toxic parent?' questionnaires a chapter heading, with some reminiscences from my LBR – Life Before Release – to give you an idea of what the signs are. You will find out in these pages that part of the toxic spiral is lies, deceit, undermining of others, self-delusion (theirs, not yours) and many other things that one person should never do to another.

I hope you can come away from this book feeling helped or at the very least, not so alone. And if so, then share that feeling. Because there are more toxic parents out there than many people realise. One short anecdote actually covers a couple of points and it goes like this:

About seven years or so ago, I was in a car accident and broke my leg. My mother was in the car with me and was unhurt. We went to hospital, leaving my mangled car behind to be towed and of course got snarled up in A&E. Because she was old and frail, they took her to X-Ray and checked her out and at no point did she mention that she was actually fine and the woman writhing in pain in the chair had perhaps got a broken leg. Finally, I too got my X-Ray and was admitted. She meanwhile had left, without saying she was going or even saying cheerio. In fact, a nurse apologised to me, saying she would have to amend my notes as she had assumed I had come in with my mother but that clearly she was just an acquaintance. If only!

Anyhow, much shenanigans later – for example, my husband had to do a couple of hundred miles by train as I had the car – I was fitted with a brace (my choice as a plaster would have meant endless physio afterwards) and kept in for a few nights before being allowed to leave. At this point I should add that mother was ringing all and sundry and saying that 'I said' I had broken my leg, but I clearly hadn't, as I didn't have a plaster on. She didn't visit while I was in, either.

At this point in the story, she would say that she bought us a replacement car. Actually, she lent us the money for a car until the insurance paid up, and it wasn't much of a car anyway – but for her, that means she was the heroine of the piece.

Back to the ward. Last night of hell on a hospital bed with nurses deaf to buzzers and the bed next to me was filled by an old lady who spent the rest of the night wailing incoherently. Morning comes none too soon, along with husband ready to spring me from prison. Almost on his heels comes the old lady's daughter and we made small talk while we waited for the painkillers to arrive, which as everyone who has ever been in hospital knows, is the longest wait on earth!

After the usual 'what did you do?' questions, I made some random polite remark about her mother. 'What a sweet old lady,' or something like that.

As soon as I had spoken, I saw that she was a fellow sufferer. 'Hmm,' she said. 'I suppose so.'

I took a risk. 'It's all right not to like your mother,' I said. 'Mine is horrible and I don't mind saying it.'

Despite the fact I was balancing very precariously on crutches, she literally flung herself into my arms and cried on my shoulder. She had been so alone, for such a long time and had no idea that others felt the way she did. Her mother was, indeed, a selfish and manipulative old bat, who had monopolised the nursing staff all night and was clearly a handful. I hope that daughter went out into the world and spread the word – that you're not alone. There is an army of us out there and we deserve a better life than our toxic parents want us to have.

I would like to say that if you think you are toxic, read on. But of course, the type of people we are talking about here wouldn't for a moment think that they are other than perfect. They will usually batten on one small thing – in my mother's case, the loan for the car, because she doesn't really understand emotions as the rest of us do – but you may find it's that babysitting they did that day (they won't have done much) or the time they looked after the cat. Ignore it. People do kind things for each other every day but don't count the cost. As Alexander Pope said, 'Do good by stealth, and blush to find it fame.' I hope I don't annoy you with quotes in this book ... hold on, of course it won't annoy you! That's a habit I have yet to break, apologising before the fact! There will be quotes, though, which I have found useful and although I am not the type to have them as embroidered samplers round my walls, I do remember them when I need them and draw comfort. Find yourself some. They won't be the same as mine, but if they speak to you, then they are doing their job.

So finally, here we go: the rest of the book. I have remained anonymous for what you will understand are good reasons. No man is an island (another quote, John Donne this time) and it wouldn't be fair if my family and friends could be identified, though they come out of this with nothing but glory. But if you want to get in touch, then please do so through my publishers, BLKDOG, to whom my most heartfelt thanks and love go.

DOES YOUR PARENT TEND TO OVERREACT OR CREATE A SCENE?

In each of the chapters that follow, I will try to find one example from my own life to illustrate the question in the chapter heading. It occurs to me as I begin with the first chapter, that it isn't always going to be easy to find just one, so please excuse me if I give a couple.

Part of being a pleasant human is to know when it isn't your day, that people are more important than you sometimes and so it's your turn to just sit down, shut up and be pleased for them.

Toxic parents can't do that. Anything that takes the limelight off them is a Bad Thing and in these situations, they usually behave pretty much like spoiled toddlers. This can be in private or in public, though it has to be said that, in the main, they prefer public. If they can conduct the whole of the scene in hissed whispers more audible than a shout, then so much the better. That way, everyone around can see how badly you have hurt them with your appalling behaviour. This behaviour may be as heinous as having the solo aged eight in your Christmas Carol Concert. Or it may be that you have left one single mouthful on your plate – you hideous ingrate, determined to bring your parents to penury by your wasteful habits. But in any event, any subsequent scene is definitely your fault. By the way, once you have children - always assuming you 'manage to find anyone willing to put up with you' - they will get sucked in to the general behaviour. And it really *really* is your job to keep them out of it, if you can. You may have to reap the whirlwind later, when they don't realise what a rancid old bat their grandmother is, but if you have done it right, they will understand, with help.

My example - as usual, hard to choose just one - actually involves one of my children. He happens to be a good musician and as a teenager played in local bands. One very exciting summer, he was playing at a local event and my parents were staying with us, partly so my dad could see him play. We spent some time at the event while he set up his stuff and my husband and I drove hither and yon picking up forgotten picks, leads and other impedimenta and then we settled down to listen. A friend of mine was there and I hope she is reading this - I'm pretty sure the evening is engraved on her brain.

They were a popular lot, so the marquee was quite full and they sang one song which was very well received. My dad was in heaven - although no singer, he did love his music and he was so proud. Throughout the song, my mother had been looking at her watch. To get the full effect, I must describe this. It involved pushing her sleeve up, raising her wrist in the air to level with her eyes and peering at it in amazement. This happened about every twenty seconds. When the applause was still ringing, she stood up, said we must be going because ... well, no one knew what it was because of, but I did. It was because someone other than her was getting applause but, worst still, I had had kisses and hugs from the rest of the band, my friend and other people who were gathered. Because I had friends. Stupid people, obviously, but I had seen the signs in the chewed lip and the thing with the watch so perhaps I was the only person there not totally gobsmacked.

My dad was gutted. She wouldn't let him stay. Our son waited until we had left, pushing past people to leave. As we got outside, I heard him say, 'We're worse than I thought. Even my grandmother can't bear to stay,' to gales of laughter. And that's why I love my son and why I say, don't let them be dragged into it.

When we got back to the house, she looked at the clock and turned on me.

'Is that the time? It's far too early. Why did you bring us back at this hour?'

I turned on my heel and left her to it. I felt bad for my dad, no gig and an evening with her malice and spite, but I knew they needed me back at the event, to clear up, derig and get everyone home. I just wish that I had stood up to her more back then, not relied on someone needing me before I did the right thing. Hindsight is a wonderful thing, isn't it? Use mine, so you don't need yours, down the line.

How to deal with it, when it happens.

Don't be like me and put up with it, which is what I usually did. Don't apologise. Don't say it's your fault *ever*. Take that phrase and chuck it out. A friend passed on a meme from somewhere online the other day and though it isn't a quote as such, here it is. 'It's time to chuck it in the f**k it bucket and move on.' Actually, if you only remember one thing from this entire book, make it this. It applies pretty much throughout. But before that, you need to deal with a potentially embarrassing and damaging situation.

If a real meltdown is on the cards, in other words, if other people, unwittingly, have fanned the flames, try to relocate. If at a gathering or somewhere, go outside or into another room. If in a supermarket or other public place, just calmly say that you can't do this here, let's go back to the car. You may well have to lead your parent away, with invective being shared with all and sundry. Remember, your toxic parent wants the world to know how awful you are.

I have never really understood this. Surely, letting

everyone know your child is ten kinds of crap makes you a not very good parent, doesn't it? This doesn't appear to have occurred to most toxic parents. All they will see, as they are led away by a blushing child of whatever age, is that everyone feels really sorry for them, saddled with this dimwit who can't even fetch them the right sort of ready meal when asked. It will help you, in this situation, to see it from the angle of the onlookers. They are thinking that that poor woman or man is having to deal with this spitting harpy (all right, I admit it, I am not going to put 'parent' each time, because the chances of it being a father are small) who is belittling her – and again, why pretend? I'll stick to mother and daughter, though I do appreciate it can be any family dynamic – and looking a bit of a fool herself. Keep calm. You'll feel better for it.

In the aftermath, you will be told it was your fault. That the scene would not have been necessary had you done whatever it was you were doing properly. The example I gave at the beginning was a complicated situation. I didn't want to ruin the evening for our son or his friends or anyone, really, so leaving was the only option. In a much more recent example, a few years ago when mother was still slightly mobile, she, my husband and I were shopping in Sainsbury's. We had almost finished, when she asked me to fetch her a shepherd's pie, which I duly did, despite the fact that we were at the far side of an enormous superstore.

'What's this?' said with much venom.

'A shepherd's pie?'

'Not this sort. Sainsbury's own.'

Back I come with a Taste the Difference or whatever the posh Sainsbury's thing is.

'What's this?'

'A shepherd's pie?'

'I'm not made of money. An ordinary one.'

This time, I come back with an ordinary Sainsbury's shepherd's pie.

'What's this?'

By this time, my husband is almost helpless with

suppressed laughter and just as well, because he kept me going at this point.

'A ... shepherd's pie?'

'You know I don't like lamb. I said cottage pie.'

Back with a cottage pie I come.

'What's this?'

By now, people are starting to loiter. One woman is literally wiping her eyes from the tears of laughter.

'A ...'

'I want two. One for the freezer.'

Back I go and come back with another. She looks at it as if it were poison.

'Where's Tom's?' Tom is her brother.

'Umm ...'

'I always get him one.'

Back I go and come back with another pie. She brandishes it triumphantly.

'What's *this*?'

'It's a cottage pie, for the love of God.'

'He always has two.'

At this point, my husband is laughing out loud as are quite a few of the loiterers. So I agree to go and get another and meet them at the till. It was funny, but not really. And one woman, as I was fuming my way down the toilet roll aisle, took me by the arm.

'I'm sorry,' she said, and pulled me in for a hug. So I suppose what this story and many others will show, is that there is always someone there who understands. My husband's laughter is our private language. He is saying 'chuck it in the f**k it bucket'. But a stranger's hug is as important, if not more so.

Bonus point in all this – when I checked my phone, I had walked over a mile and a half. In Sainsbury's! Who says cottage pie isn't healthy?

When you decide it's time to go ...

Whatever your age, you have probably lived through many experiences of bad behaviours when a simple remark or comment causes a real stream of invective. You have rolled with the punches, perhaps talking back occasionally and then – of course – apologising later as if it is all your fault. The rule here – and throughout this journey we are on, really – is that it is *not* your fault. Okay, every argument has two sides, but the chances are that you are so flattened by your toxic parent that you are not that often in the wrong. Simple self-preservation has taught you not to argue or even contradict her. If she has an adequate audience, she will belittle you for the smallest thing, usually smiling smugly at the others there. Secret coming up – they aren't stupid, these people. But a toxic parent isn't just a toxic parent. They are toxic, full stop. And so it is likely that the audience will also go along with it, for a quiet life – this particularly applies to family members, who walk on eggshells just like you do.

But finally, a day will come when the over-reaction and subsequent drama just isn't something you want to deal with. For me, this came in a phone call – thank you, COVID-19, I knew your cloud had a silver lining – when enough was suddenly enough. I heard myself saying, over the whining and self-justification, 'Just shut up, mother, and listen.' The sheer surprise stopped her in her tracks and I was able to tell her exactly what I thought of her. Because of her dementia, she probably forgot about almost immediately, but I haven't. It felt good and although if she calls I will answer, I won't be dialling her number ever again.

Stepping back isn't easy but it isn't good for anyone to have to pussyfoot around in case another person over-reacts or makes a scene. It isn't just horrible for you but also for any onlookers, who will be invited, either overtly or covertly by your toxic parent, to take sides. Families and friendships have been irretrievably broken in this way and the question you have to ask is – 'Is it worth it?' Perhaps in some settings, such as Sainsbury's, the answer is yes, let's just get the next five minutes sorted and get out of here. In the case of friends and family – no. One person you don't like set against the rest of the world? A no brainer. You may need to just step away and contact people one-to-one later to explain your choice. They will either understand or they won't. But honestly, if they choose the path of toxicity, do you want them in your life at all?

Disassociating yourself either completely or partially from your toxic parent isn't something to do lightly. Like me, there may come a breaking point and then the decision is made for you. For others, it will be a long, slow, drip, drip, drip of venom and spite but even in that case, the day will come. I was pretty near it when she took the decision out of my hands. In a way, that was fortunate, because everyone understood more easily. But really, if you find yourself waking up every morning dreading a phone call or personal encounter, get the hell out!

But before you do ...

Not every melting down parent is toxic. It's important in all this to remember that sometimes, parents are just people, going through the same shit as everyone else and perhaps just not sharing it the way they should. So, if the over-reactions and tantrums are of recent onset *or*, given a moment's thought you can see the reason for them, even though it's a bit of a stretch sometimes, you probably don't have a toxic parent. You have a parent who could do with a hug or a bit of a chat. Not everyone can share when they are feeling overwhelmed, so, as a child, be patient. And also, think whether perhaps it was justified this once. Or even twice. None of these categories marks a toxic parent if it is the only one that applies. It is a pattern, not a single event. Everyone wants shot of a family member sometimes – just make sure that it isn't a kneejerk reaction on your part and be prepared to dig a little deeper.

So, before heading for the hills, have a little think. Has this been happening all your life? Or just last Saturday when

you turned up late and pissed just once too many times?
    Just saying.

DOES YOUR PARENT USE EMOTIONAL BLACKMAIL?

As with all the questions in this book, the obvious answer here is 'Hell, yeah!' But it isn't always as obvious as you might think. When picturing someone using emotional blackmail, the non-toxic parent owner might think it goes something like 'you don't love me' 'Of course I do' and that's it, done and dusted. But no. It's far more subtle than that. When faced with what they see as insubordination (because don't forget, the toxic parent's abiding mantra is that you should never be out of their control), they will drag up a tiny thing from the past and make it into something it isn't. Usually you have forgotten about it, so minor was it, but no guilt trip is too big or too small for the toxic parent. Often, finances rear their head. It's also personal sacrifices they made for you, of which you were probably unaware.

I was a bright kid and got into the prestigious girls' grammar school in a town not that easy to reach by bus, but it was just possible. I had to leave the house at 8 o'clock every morning and got home around 5.30, that is if the buses all worked. Fortunately, I went to my grandparents' house every morning on the way to the bus stop, having given my brother his breakfast first of course, and my Nana gave me stuff for break. In the evening, I went there again for an evening meal. They were bright spots of love and care in the day and I still thank God for those wonderful people. My uncle lived with them and he was a piece of work as well, but let's leave him out of it, for now.

I was a bit gobsmacked by 'big school' but, as I said, I was a bright kid, so did well at first. Then the emotional blackmail began. While I was 'getting ideas above my station', while I was 'getting posh', my mother, apparently, was working her fingers to the bone in order to ... what? I saw nothing that would account for this apparent industry. I was given a pencil case by an aunt and that was it. When the pen ran out, there wasn't one in the house. I know that seems weird now. Sitting here typing and barely moving my head, I can see six biros and I know we have drawers with dozens more. When it came to doing my homework – several hours of it a night at the age of eleven – and no pen to do it with, I was told tough luck. There were better things to spend money on than stupid pens. So, no homework done until I could borrow a pen at school next day.

Then, it turned out, all this working to provide me with nothing at all was wearing her out so much that she couldn't put my brother to bed. Six years younger than me and very challenging due to various learning difficulties, it became my job. I had very long hair then and I would have to go to bed with him until he fell asleep; snag was, he would wind his hands in my hair so I couldn't leave. So, no homework done and no letter or kind phone call to explain to the school why.

If I was lucky enough to do my homework, then my brother would also be brought into the mix. We had no paper or crayons in the house and it wasn't fair, was it, that I, with brains and a pencil case, had all the fun. So he was allowed to scribble and tear and generally lay waste to my books. So, no homework done and again, no explanation to get me out of the soup.

Scroll on to the end of year exams, where, surprise, surprise, I didn't exactly shine. In fact, with an IQ of 150+, I came bottom of ninety other girls. I was gutted, as were the teachers who I know had had high hopes of me. Our school broke up at lunchtime on the last day of term so I got back home while my mother was on her own in the house. The letter from school had already arrived and so I walked in to icy silence.

I was all kinds of ungrateful little bitch. How dare I make her look stupid like this? Can I add here that she had attended no parents' evenings, had responded to none of the concerned letters the school had been sending, had shown no interest at all in my progress thus far. Had I no idea what she had given up so I could attend this school? No, actually, and to this day I still have no idea. Whatever would the neighbours say? Nothing, as she didn't speak to them as far as I knew, and they certainly had no knowledge of my school report. How could I break her heart this way? I was selfish and ungrateful and if I didn't pull my socks up, she would probably become ill with the worry of it all.

Then she hit me upside the head with the iron, but that belongs somewhere else in this book, I think.

The upshot of this, of course, was that nothing whatsoever changed. My brother still ruled my academic life and I still did appallingly badly at school. It's no good being bright and understanding every single thing in every lesson if your homework doesn't appear or looks like the dog has been at it and revision for exams is ten minutes grabbed on the bus. My grandparents, loving as they were, didn't really understand the whole academic thing and anyway, had a habit borne of years of experience, of appeasing my mother. Like I said, toxic parents aren't just toxic to their children. Like mould on bread, their influence is much wider than the obvious green splodge of hatred and manipulation that shows on the surface.

Scroll on a few years and I got a job in London which I admit wouldn't have been my first choice, but I grew to love it and it did okay by me for the rest of the century. I didn't even consider university, partly because of my woeful A Level results but mainly because the fingers were still being worked to the bone, apparently, and it was made clear that supporting me a moment longer would bring death and destruction. It's no good saying that my life would have been different had I done the subjects I wanted to and gone to university, yadda, yadda, because who knows what life would be like down, in the words of the late, great Terry Pratchett, the other trouser leg of time. Suffice to say, had my grandparents not been still alive at that point, I would have started running then and not stopped until my legs gave out.

But, well, I am the nice one, to quote Ralph Richardson in *Time Bandits,* so I carried on going home for another hammering – by now, happily, only verbal – for years. And years. And years.

One thing you have to remember when it comes to emotional blackmailers, they lie. Well, toxic parents always lie, it is their default position, but when employing emotional blackmail, they can lie on an Olympic scale. Everything you have ever done, from birth possibly – in my case before, as I made the fundamental error of actually coming into being as a result of my mother's dalliance with a passing soldier with a wife somewhere – will be trotted out and listed as the reason why she is now in such a parlous state, usually of health. So, my schooldays were not blighted by a feral brother and lack of support but because I was out every night with boys without number. This little titbit was actually told to one of our children, to her and my great surprise. Actually, I had my first boyfriend at sixteen and then two more before my husband. If that's promiscuous, it isn't the definition usually given to the word. Because of this appalling behaviour, apparently, she would stand anxiously at the window, plucking fretfully at the curtains until I wove my unsteady way up the path, thus making her exhausted because of the working her fingers to the bone, etc.

To put some flesh on the bones of my dating habits, should I be fortunate enough to be allowed out – often rescinded at the last moment, because of my brother-sitting duties – I had to be home by 9.30 at the latest. This meant some interesting cinema visits. What we had to do – and I must have had very patient boyfriends – was go to the end of the first sitting and then watch the film round to the point where we went in (you could do that then). I am therefore one of the few people who knew that the Planet of the Apes was Earth before Charlton Heston set foot on it and that Bonnie and Clyde die in a hail of bullets before they even meet. It made following plots a little tricky sometimes. Don't get me started on *Bob and Carol and Ted and Alice*.

If I were to be five minutes late, my dad was sent to stand at the gate, like something out of an old John Wayne movie, anxiously scanning the horizon for my return. When I got home, the silent treatment was the norm, followed by loving nuggets of information like no wonder my boyfriend was so ugly – to be fair, one was a little odd-looking, but generally, they polished up okay – because who else would go out with me. Modesty forbids, but I didn't turn milk, either. Then we would get onto the real subject of the evening. How could I leave her to deal with my brother on her own? Easily should have been my answer, but I didn't know I could, then. My homework would have suffered, of course. Because she couldn't be everywhere. She was working her fingers ... have I said this already? That's something you will find with the emotional blackmailer. They find a good thing and by and large, they stick by it.

Blackmail can be just blackmail

Emotional blackmail is easy, of course, because it doesn't have to make any sense at all. But sometimes, the toxic parent uses straight up, old fashioned blackmail. I think I have already said that my grandparents and I were a tight little unit and of course, thank goodness for them, because without them, I wouldn't be the approaching normal person I am today. But I know that she used me as a pawn in her game, to stop them even criticising her; 'if you don't do/do such and such, you won't see your granddaughter ever again'. She even went so far as to start the process of emigrating to New Zealand, with no intention of doing it, to scare them witless.

Blackmail, literal or emotional, is probably one of the worst things a person can do to another. It shows a complete lack of care for that other person, an absence of empathy as to how the person you are supposed to love will be feeling. I can remember my grandfather sitting in his greenhouse with tears running down his cheeks, just holding my hand. That's a lot for a six-year-old to take in and something they shouldn't really see. Which is not to say, I must hurriedly add, that crying in front of children is wrong – it's the way they learn that emotions are okay. No, a man of sixty sitting alone in a greenhouse, in the twilight, silently crying because of something done to him by his own daughter ... That's twenty kinds of wrong.

We all do it sometimes ...

I don't think there is a person alive who hasn't resorted to a little emotional blackmail, hopefully normally with a twinkle in their eye.

My mother-in-law, a bit of a handful but not really toxic, used to have the pleasure of her son's company every single school holiday after her husband died. Yes, folks, every single one. And at the end of each visit, she would sigh, roll her eyes heavenward and mutter, 'Well, thank you for coming, anyway.' Without the 'anyway', it's a thank you. With it, emotional blackmail. Sometimes, words matter.

'If you loved me, you would fetch me a gin and tonic' is okay, because no one is being staked out over an anthill and made to feel dreadful because of it. And anyhow, normally, the blackmailee is gagging for a drink as well about now, so no harm, no foul.

'If you loved me, you would buy me a computer' is slightly different. Something expensive – or not bought, but difficult to achieve, such as working shorter hours, that kind of thing – is not a topic for banter blackmail. Discuss the purchase, change, without the 'if you loved me' bit, if you don't want to be toxic.

The toxic parent is unlikely to start any conversation like this, however, because, however you slice it, the only person they love is themselves. Full stop.

Alex Farrell

DOES YOUR PARENT MAKE FREQUENT OR UNREASONABLE DEMANDS?

This is one of the few boxes that not everyone ticks. Some toxic parents get a lot of pleasure for not asking for anything, then responding with a heavy sigh when something isn't done, that really, they didn't like to ask, poor little old them is so unworthy – see emotional blackmail for that little trick. Others ask for everything, from doing the shopping to driving miles in order to take them somewhere that is cancelled when you get there. 'I didn't want to be a trouble ...' is usually the excuse there and we're back to the old E.B. again.

The toxic parent has, by the time their child is grown up and probably with children of their own, had thirty years or so to hone their skills, so it doesn't faze them for one second that said child has their own responsibilities. When my children were small, I had an extremely responsible job – yes, me! However did I manage it; probably slept with the HR manager, what do you reckon? – and sometimes needed help with childcare. This was never really that possible, because of ... and again, insert any pathetic excuse you can think of. In fact, my mother helped me once, just once, in all my childcare needing days, and that was because I had a role in a large local event and so she could stand beaming at my elbow, basking in reflected glory. And God, can that woman bask! This is a common part of the toxic parent's behaviour and the only time their child is considered worthwhile. Once the basking stops, then they are back to being worthless scum who ruined their lives.

But despite their antipathy to helping out, no matter how dire the need, the unreasonable demand is right up there on their to do list. This generally happens when they get older and hospital visits and their like start coming over the horizon. It won't matter that their child has children of their own, a job, a life even – though, in the eyes of the toxic parent this is unlikely, because who would want to be friends with a loser like you? If they need to go to the doctor or hospital, then you have to be there. Otherwise (and here comes the emotional blackmail again) they will have to ask a neighbour to do it. And what would people think?

This is an easier one to cope with than many. If you live nearby, chances are you can actually manage most of these hospitally things. And if you don't, what the hell do you care what the neighbours think? Let them do it – your back is broad and you really shouldn't give it another thought.

In the light of recent events re my mother, I checked back in my email inbox and discovered – to my surprise, I may say – that I have been turning myself inside out to make sure she is kept safe and well and doesn't become a victim of her health denial for over six years! I had no idea that this part of our relationship had ruled my life for so long. I have never, ever had a word of thanks – but, remember Alexander Pope, people; that's not why I do it – or acknowledgement. Worse, recently, her sister has climbed on the denial bandwagon and now I am fighting a battle on two fronts. Actually, make that 'fought' because I have now taken my contact details off every list – she's someone else's problem now.

But in one year, we were at home for never longer than

ten days, interspersed with visits to her, or 'home' as her brother liked to call it. It wasn't 'home' even when I had no other, so it certainly isn't now. Make sure in all this that that is made crystal clear. You are not going 'home' to do what you are asked. You are visiting your mother or father in theirs. It isn't their right. You are doing them a favour. Also, you will need to make sure that neighbours don't have you on a piece of string. They don't want responsibility for your ghastly relation and indeed, why the hell should they? I am now an only child, my brother having died some time ago. Siblings are dealt with in their own chapter, but it is often the case that one child in a family can be a 'scapegoat' child. If this is you, you have my sympathy. My mother was pretty generous in her toxicity, so I never felt that singled out. Her behaviour to my brother was different but in many ways, more insupportable. However, the siblings chapter for that.

In the conversation that we had running up to my final epiphany and stepping back, of course, money came up. Her dementia is now quite bad sometimes, but the day she lent me 4/3d for an ice cream is still very clear in her mind. The fact she lent me £4k last year and every year before from time immemorial is also clear, just, sadly, fiction. However, many people fall for it and here again, the broad back comes into play. Far from having untold riches from her, one year we spent almost £9k on travel alone. Did I say we don't live near? Are you surprised?

But no matter what the cost to you, either in money or cancelled events, holidays, even, the demands will continue. 'Can you just get me ...?' 'Can you just take me ...?' 'Can you arrange ...?' all sound like reasonable requests. But in fact, the 'can you' bit is just window dressing. There is no option built in at all. You *will* do this thing, or the emotional blackmail will kick in, the scenes if you are physically present, the exaggerated lies to friends and relatives if you are not. For more years than I care to remember, I danced to the tune of 'can you'? More recently, my husband has also got sucked in – for years after my broken leg, I was not a confident driver and so he would come as well.

One story will suffice for this one and most children of toxic parents will have something almost exactly similar. One weekend, when we were both working still, so quite important down time, we had a phone call from mother, saying her leg 'wasn't working' and she was stuck in the bedroom. Obviously, from a distance, we couldn't do anything to unstick her from the bedroom, but I made some calls, got the immediate problem dealt with, packed a bag, arranged for someone to feed the cats and sped off.

Imagine our surprise on arriving, to find her sitting on the sofa, laughing and joking with a woman from down the road, *legs crossed, swinging the 'bad' leg happily.* I could hardly speak, and my husband was all for leaving there and then. So, I asked her what was going on.

'It's me leg.' I will render her speech as verbatim, because she adopts this strange patois when speaking to me. 'It went funny.'

'But it's all right now?'

'Yes. But you were on your way.'

'You could have let me know.'

'I don't know your mobile number.'

'Yes, you do, you *rang me on it.*'

'Did I? Oh. Well, you're here now. How long you stopping?'

The answer was, as long as it took to turn the car around. There was no argument on that particular occasion, but there should have been. We just left, for damage limitation, but looking back, we should have torn her a new one and backed off then as we now have. Because, in a way, she saw it as validation for shouting whenever she wanted to pull the string. And because of some underlying health issues she has, it has been hard to ignore her when she complains of dizziness ('I was that sick and bad') or inability to swallow (vile retching noises on the phone).

When a toxic parent combines the emotional blackmail tool with an unreasonable request, you have to be strong and keep on saying no. Yes, the neighbours will hear all about your selfishness – don't forget all those thousands of pounds she gives you every year – and how you don't care. But why should that bother you? And the answer is, it shouldn't.

Special days are always fair game for a toxic parent. You *must* come for Mother's Day. I got that one year and I pointed out I was a mother as well and so was being taken out. This was treated with disdain. I could be taken out on any day of the year, this was *Mother's* Day. What was I not understanding? So, I said again that, as a mother, I was being taken out, table all booked, the works. On this particular year, the phone was slammed down and I spent the next hour trying to ring back. I would like to say to that me of all those years ago – what were you *thinking*? I didn't ask to be taken out – my children sprang it as a surprise. If I too had had to demand a Sunday lunch, then I would have been as toxic as her. But hopefully, I have avoided that minefield.

This year has been particularly difficult for the child of a toxic parent. With pictures in every newspaper of weeping grannies touching their grandchildren's palms through the windows of nursing homes, the toxic parent starts to get antsy when they aren't getting the same. Essentially, toxic parent, in time of plague, people only go the extra mile for those who deserve it, and you don't. It would be good if this were to be a learning curve, as they see other people getting dressed up in plastic or constructing a sentry box gizmo so they can see their loved ones. You, toxic parent, are not a loved one, so you'll have to wait it out. Of course I have had the emotional blackmail ('I don't see nobody') and the unreasonable demand ('Are you coming to stop at Christmas?') and then more emotional blackmail in case I missed the first bit – my uncle died last year and despite the fact that he spent about half an hour with her as he hoovered up his Christmas dinner and then threw a screwed up tenner at her as a present (I told you he was a piece of work), apparently he 'made Christmas' for her and she doesn't know how she'll cope. Okay, I guess.

If not, no longer my problem.

As Christmas has reared its head, let's just have a word about it. It's one day. Spend it with who you want. Don't uproot yourself and your kids to go and spend it with someone who won't like the present, won't like your take on the mighty Brussels Sprout, won't want to play games and if they do, they have to win – basically, all the Christmas clichés. Do what *you* want at Christmas. Toxicity is for life, not just for Christmas, sadly, so give yourself a break.

Ho, ho, ho.

When is a demand unreasonable and how do you tell?

Obviously, some medical needs are urgent and you have to use your judgement. If the call comes from a professional, then it is usually genuine and then it's up to you. I have now taken the step of passing on my mother's day to day care calls to someone else, but for years, I was frontline, making sure the care package was right for her and happening, all that kind of thing. I would dash to and fro to get her to appointments, to find she had arranged a neighbour to do it and didn't 'want to annoy them' so I was left sitting in the house while some old geezer almost as infirm as her took her instead. Only you know the needs of your toxic parent, so if the demand sounds a bit dodgy, check it with the hospital/GP etc. They probably won't talk about it in detail, but most will tell you if an appointment exists.

If the demand is that you go and take her shopping, to get her hair done, to be in while the carpet man calls, tell her to do the other thing. You have a life, remember? Use it on yourself, not your toxic parent. The daughter of an acquaintance of my mother (I won't say friend, because she doesn't have any as most of us understand them) has to ring her mother at ten every morning wherever she is in the world. So, when she went on holiday to California, she had to set an alarm for two in the morning or something dumb like that, so as to make the call. That woman is a doormat. Her mother is beyond toxic. Don't be that person – you will never, if you live to be a thousand, get a word of thanks.

Another side to the unreasonable demands is that you will take their side, no matter what depths of unreasonable bigotry they descend to. Live and let live, that's my motto (to quote the Major in *Fawlty Towers* for a moment there) and so people are as free to have their opinions as I am, whatever they may be. But sometimes, when they are wrong on almost everyone's radar, you have to take a stand. My mother is, like many of her generation, spectacularly racist, using epithets I am not going to write down, not even with asterisks. She often tried to get me to agree with her views, but this was one ditch I was prepared to die in. Almost literally once or twice, as she would say the derogatory words very loudly when in mixed race company. Once, when we were passing a group of lads in a town centre, one stepped up to me and I was a bit worried – but no, he gave me a hug and a pat which said 'Solidarity!' I've had a few of those, but none that caused her quite the heebie jeebies that one did. Once, I bought my husband a coat from an Asian guy in a market. He was exactly the same build as my husband so I got him to try it on for me and he did, twirling and doing the catwalk thing. It was *perfect* so I got him to bag it up for me. Yells from mother, 'Don't have that one! That old … … has had it on!' Lovely chap, he started to take it out of the bag, but I stopped him. When we got home, she tried to wash the coat, took it outside to brush it and everything – needless to say, my husband wore it all the time. Until he left it behind in a service station years later, but this book isn't about daffy husbands, so we will leave that story there.

Alex Farrell

DOES YOUR PARENT TRY TO CONTROL YOU?

Hell, yes.

Oh, do you need more? Perhaps the defining part of a toxic parent's character is that they are controlling and not usually just of you. This is somewhere where you and the rest of the family meet. Even if you are the scapegoat, then the toxic parent can't just control you, she has to control the lot. The world, for preference. If she works outside the home in a position of even slight responsibility, she will be in charge of that workplace. She will insist on her methods of filing, her methods of storing the mugs, the biscuits, the tea towels – there is no detail too small for the toxic parent and having honed her skills on you, that workplace had better watch out!

My own particular toxic parent has no qualifications or noticeable skills, although of course the stories of former glories were well-worn and always left her in a good light. So she had limited workplace control opportunities. She therefore fell back on the 'everyone loves me at work' thing, often pressing her ... actually this is making me feel a little queasy ... self, shall we say, upon the boss, even into her seventies. Especially her gay boss, but we'll go no further into that. Even from her lowly position, she could dominate though. One story will suffice.

She worked in a service industry and insisted on

providing desserts for her place of work to sell, Sundays only. When my dad was dying, she didn't want to go to the hospital because 'they need me puddin's' – again the strange patois, can anyone explain that? – so I shoved her out of the door and made them myself.

I took them to her place of work, and I could see faces falling even while I was opening the boot to get them out. Her boss came out with hands extended, saying really, no, she shouldn't have bothered, not with ... And here he stopped. Because instead of grey bread and butter pudding with five dead fly currants there was a dish of my signature baguette and marmalade bread and butter pudding, light as a cloud and all out gorgeous (say it myself as shouldn't, because of course, I can't cook for toffee, can I?), a couple of tiramisus and a giant tarte tatin. He took them into the kitchen and came out with the cash (she had never mentioned she was paid!) and said thank you, how long was I staying, what about next week? Sadly, I wasn't staying and he blurted out that they threw her food away, because no one could actually eat it and they had had complaints. Did I tell her? No. Did they? Nope to that as well, because, bottom line, we are all enablers of the control freaks that we live with, for a quiet life.

It's doubtful that a child of a toxic parent will be aware of the level of control until they move away, assuming they manage it. It's only when you put some distance between you and start making your own decisions that you can see how much every second of every day of your life was under their control. And woe betide you if you try to change a moment of it. Because of my career choice, I am now super flexible because I had to be, but I do realise that without that retraining, I would probably be living a life as if it ran on rails. Don't do that, do this because ... well, there is never a real reason. Just because and often – in my case certainly – a bit of reinforcement with a smack upside the head, for insubordination.

When control becomes a danger and how to spot the

moment

The main thing to be aware of – and the sooner the better – is that your toxic parent doesn't know it all. Unlike mine, yours may be educated to a further level and actually be quite bright, but even they won't know it *all.* There will be many bits of life where they have no actual experience and so letting them rule your choices of career, partner, location etc is plain dumb. But they will also poke their noses – and fingers – into everything. Lump in breast? Don't worry. Your grandmother had that and she lived to be a hundred and ten. This is not my experience, by the way, but that of a dear friend who died because of it. She lived in middle age with her toxic, controlling mother who literally through force of will stopped her from getting medical care. And then badmouthed her till her own dying day for leaving her to look after herself when she should have been her carer in old age. Car making a weird noise and pulling to the left when you brake? No problem (they often can't drive), everyone's does that and until you are squashed by an oncoming truck, they won't say otherwise. And of course, post squashing, you will be cursed up hill and down for being a crap driver. Abdominal swelling, yellow eyes and night sweats. A virus. Or, as happened in the case of my brother, colon cancer with ascites and liver secondaries. I can't even talk about that – so to sum up, they don't know anything. Ignore them as soon as you are old enough to do so. And get the hell out – good advice for any section in this book, really.

Does your parent belittle, criticize or compare you?

If a child of a toxic parent is asked to say what the worst thing is, it would be this. No matter what you do or how well you do it, you won't be as good as the neighbour, their kid or, in extreme cases, their cat. Let's put my cards on the table. I have a stable and happy marriage, a wonderful family down to the very last grandchild. They are also super happy, nice, talented and successful. Whether on the creative side or more practical (and some of us are both), we are pretty good. I cook, knit, crochet, sew and, before I married an artist much better than me, draw. The kids are musical to varying degrees, artistic, inspired in their careers. Before you write me off as a big-headed waste of space, let me let you into a little secret – before putting my mother in the f**k it bucket, I would have died rather than write the above. Because I was worthless. Ugly, fat, probably stupid, the worst mother/wife/grandmother/pet owner on the planet. If you're told it enough, you'll believe it.

    Slight side issue here. Toxicity often affects a whole generation. My uncle, God help us all, was even worse than my mother, but didn't marry or have children and with that small gap between us, could do less harm, though he tried, my word, how he tried. Their sister, the baby of the family, is not quite as bad, but she brings more inventiveness to it. She has told me, with a straight face and apparent concern, that she is sorry that I am jealous of her grandson, who is so marvellous when my son is such a disappointment. Her sheer effrontery takes your breath away but without breath there is no response, so she goes on her way rejoicing. This same person, when her brother was alive and well but had had a touch of flu, told me 'You don't know what it's like to lose a brother.' Umm ... I kinda do ...

    The toxic belittler does love to gather her forces and so, if she has a bone to pick, she usually will make sure she has back-up. For a while, for my mother, it was a neighbour who went in with a friendly cup of coffee and ended up being almost taken hostage. Every opinion of mine was passed by her (or probably it wasn't, she would just invoke her name regardless) and any gift, in particular, would be greeted with 'I carn make it out. Gloria cou'dn' make it out nyther.' As the last gift before Gloria did a runner and slammed the door behind her was a mug and spoon, I somehow doubt that that was right. But if you can rely on one thing, you can rely on the fact that common sense will never be a big feature in your parent's attempts to belittle.

Anyway, back to the main point, does your parent criticize or compare you? Yes, of course, is the answer.

How to deal with it.

This one is tricky because depending on the level of vitriol, it might be possible to just walk away muttering in your head about what a bitch, but sometimes, and especially in public, it can be very upsetting. To engage means that you engage the other person and remember, this isn't their fault. They are probably as mortified as you are. This is one of these that really does rely on you to take the moral high ground and just walk away, even if it means leaving her talking to fresh air. Because let's face it, if she drives you to walk away forever, she will be doing a lot of that. Might as well get used to it sooner as later.

When has it gone too far?

A lot of this depends on what you do for a living, whether your public reputation matters to your lifestyle and job. My mother was never in a position to harm my professional reputation, so it really has never been that important, except from a self esteem point of view. But if you are, for instance, a local retailer or specialist like a hairdresser or medical professional, it can matter a lot and that is when you need to draw a line. Tell her that if you hear that she has been criticising your professional standards, you will need to call your solicitor. That will be met with poo-pooing noises, but don't falter. A warning letter is something she has probably deserved for years anyway!

Funny story, though – and if you take just one thing away from this, make it the fact that without a sense of humour you are *toast* – is something that happened some years ago, when she was at least a little mobile. Someone on the village hall committee had for some reason taken it into their head to have a chicken dinner evening, with entertainment from a Bargain Hunt expert (not a current one) and so I decided to go along, as BH was at the time my guilty pleasure. The whole thing was a disaster, the meal wasn't ready and everyone just milled around aimlessly and pretty much ignoring the poor expert, who most of them didn't know from a bar of soap. I went up to him and started chatting and of course, that was all kinds of wrong and so mother came along as well, to make sure she could insert herself into the conversation and hopefully, as a happy side effect, make me look small.

She rather over-reached herself on this occasion as antiques are a bit of a thing for me and I could chat quite knowledgably with the guy and soon we were getting along like houses on fire. She was a bit stumped when it came to adding to a conversation based around arts and crafts furniture, collecting of, and so decided to actually physically remove me, by pulling on my sleeve and kind of half pulling, half pushing me away. The expert was a little baffled but decided to join in the fun, so followed me, keeping the exact same distance between us and the conversation running smoothly. And, love the man, he continued to do so when she added her special super power to the mix and began to fart – probably from the effort. Eventually, the dinner was ready and we all settled down to listen to his talk, but he kept giving me sidelong glances and we both had difficulty keeping a straight face. And the moral of this story is, always bear in mind that other people can spot that she is a bit 'off' (not because of the smell, I think the farting is a bit of a niche thing) but because her behaviour, which has become the norm for you, is not the norm for 90% of the population. Raise your eyes from your accustomed position of horrified embarrassment and you will see that almost everyone gets the picture and know it's not you, it's her.

Alex Farrell

DOES YOUR PARENT LISTEN TO YOU WITH INTEREST?

Of course the answer to this one is no. She will never have listened to a single voice in her life except her own. I have grandsons now and hang on their every word. Okay, much of it is football or how to get past level 3 in Sonic the Hedgehog (or whatever, it's hard to keep track) but I do listen, ask intelligent questions and let the conversation go where it will. I was the same with my children. I hope I am the same with everyone I meet, because I am of the opinion that the chances are they have something interesting to say. A toxic parent does not think that. Two scenarios here. Your toxic parent may be, like mine, someone with little education – sidebar, this is my fault, for being born, although she was 20 at the time and had already made the decision to take a job filling doughnuts with jam in the canteen of a local car factory – and so not interested in anything anyway. Or they may be intelligent and to the outside world a super-level listener. The bottom line on this one is; it won't matter which they are, because the only interesting thing is a thing they are talking about.

I write books for a living. This isn't actually super interesting to anyone because the act of writing is really quite solitary, it is the finished article that is the interesting bit.

However, a while ago I went off piste a bit and ghosted a book by quite a famous person who wanted their childhood fantasy written down as a novel for adults. It was tricky, but I got it done and I thought that this might be interesting, as it is quite unusual. I started to tell her and she literally got up and wandered out of the room, not to go to the loo or make a cup of tea, but just to sit in another room. The problem for her here was that she wasn't going to be able to turn the story to something that had happened to her. She would just have to listen and perhaps at the end, praise me. She was so bewildered by these choices that she had no recourse but to get up and leave. This is just one example, she often did that; this was just the most blatant. People who are more than usually forgiving may say that she was already in the first stages of dementia but actually (although she may have been) this has absolutely no bearing on her reaction to me telling her something she couldn't turn. She had been doing it all my life. Had a good day at school – nothing like as good as her good days, which were so amazing that the teacher accompanied her home to tell her parents. Bad day? Good grief, nothing like as bad as hers, which were turned into a mini series (slight exaggeration there, but you get my drift).

Not everything you want to share – or once upon a time wanted to share, because the sharing thing soon drops of the list of things you bother with – is a good story. Sometimes, you want to share something that troubles you, or you would like advice on. But again, you are wasting your breath, because after the first few sentences, you will be shut down or the story will be capped.

What to do if they won't listen

Do what I did and simply stop sharing. The toxic parent hates nothing more than to be told how well you are doing, how interesting you are, by a third party when they don't know what that person is talking about. A marvellous parent like them surely has a child who shares everything. Well, no, actually – they don't. Because thirty years or so of being walked out on mid-sentence makes you a bit more tight-lipped. I always took knitting or, better still, a laptop, and would simply sit in the same room on visits, not uttering a single syllable.

They hate that! Because they are the most important person in the room, clearly you want to tell them all about your life. But play the silence game. It is fun and if you can turn anything in your relationship with your toxic parent into a fun thing, grab the opportunity, because they don't come around that often.

I was once sitting, with my husband, watching some god-awful reality show at my mother's house. It 'starred' Ant and Dec (of course) and we were chatting about the possible winner. A slight sidebar here – because of the layout of her room, only she could see the whole TV screen, so other people could only see, to continue the example, Ant *or* Dec. I think I had Ant on this occasion. Anyhow, there we were, chatting away about who ate crocodile testicles with the most aplomb when she switched off the TV, got up, switched off the light and left the room, shutting the door behind her.

We sat there for a moment and I can't remember which of us asked the question, 'What just happened?' And the answer was, of course, that she had lost interest in us, Ant and Dec and reptilian knick-knacks and so it was clearly time for bed.

This was a later example of other behaviours such as clearing the table when I was chatting to my dad after tea, hoovering suddenly in the middle of a chat about my new job and the other myriad times when for once she wasn't able to turn the conversation to be about her.

Will She Ever Listen?

No.

DOES YOUR PARENT MANIPULATE, USE GUILT, OR PLAY THE VICTIM?

You are probably getting used to the answers to all these questions, which will always be, of course, yes. This one, though, is the clincher as to whether you have a toxic parent or just one who is a bit needy. I think in our lives most of us use a bit of emotional blackmail (see the chapter with that very title) but the toxic parent takes it beyond that. The manipulation is very subtle sometimes and you hardly know it has happened until you look back and think 'Wait! What the ...?' This manipulation is often centred on annual events, such as Christmas, birthdays, Mother's Day etc. My mother's speciality was Easter. Easter cards, mainly. This is not, let me say, because of any deep religious feeling. The cards were covered in spring flowers and bunnies, not joy that Christ is risen. Failure to send an Easter card was almost a hanging offence.

Fast forward through the many years when by fair means or foul she would somehow inveigle us to visit her for Easter, only to have us sit there in misery with no Egg Hunt, no Easter Bunny, no ... no anything. Because, although of course Easter was a 'holiday', when push came to shove, she had no idea how to have a good time, if it didn't involve some rather stomach-churning gurning at men young enough to be her sons (and later, grandsons) and a moderate amount of Pernod. This is not to say she was a heavy drinker, she wasn't, but this was her classic 'night out'. I think the choice of Pernod says a lot – who drinks that unless it is to draw attention? A bright orange drink is going to do that, isn't it?

So, after a good old while, my son and I joined a church choir, quite a hardcore one, with a full anthem every Sunday, and at Easter we really pushed the boat out. He was head chorister. I was a kind of 'choir mother', ironing the ruffs, taking the little dears out when they had a wobble, all that. So at Easter, we went through from on Maundy Thursday to all day on Good Friday, ending with evensong – still my favourite service in the year – through Holy Saturday and into Easter Sunday, hours and hours of services, all with big production number singing. We did that for a total of seven Easters and for every single one the attempt at manipulation would begin in about February. I held firm, because we were, without blowing my own trumpet, kind of lynchpins to making a very heavy four days of services work at all. She was incandescent every year and one, she agreed to come to us. I wasn't happy, because I was pretty sure she would manage to wreck it somehow, but my dad wanted to hear us sing, so I relented.

Picture the scene. It is Holy Saturday and her grandson is singing his first tenor solo in a complex piece of Russian plainsong, heartbreakingly beautiful.

You've guessed it, haven't you? You've been with me a while now, so you know. Yup! She walked out, with much bumping into pew ends and dropping of hymn books. I do give my dad full marks though – this was one time when he didn't scurry after her and although he doubtless got it in the neck later, good on him.

So you have to watch it when dealing with manipulation. If you think you have won, you probably haven't, because the toxic parent has more than one string to their bow.

How to cope with it

Don't give in is the easy answer. Because you will find, like I did, that they will always find a way to spoil the alternative that replaced their plans. It could be as simple as walking out, but it could be worse. My husband and I used to lecture on cruises and I think I can count on the fingers of one hand the times we did one without an attempt at the beginning to stop us going – 'I feel that sick and bad' – or our return being to an urgent message at customs – 'Your mother has had to be taken into hospital. She was apparently that sick and bad.' At first, we would react, but towards the end many a customs official was a bit startled by my casual shrug. Except the ones with a toxic parent. They understood all right.

You will see from the above examples that really manipulation includes guilt trips and victimhood. Other examples in the book – 'I work my fingers to the bone' being a classic – sum up the situation well. The lesson to take away, really, is that this is all just part of the big plan. They don't want you, and often make no bones about it – 'Having you ruined my life/stopped my education/made me ill and I wish you had never been born' – but on the other hand, they don't want anyone else to have you either – 'You're too fat/ugly/stupid to ever find anyone to love you.' To them, you are like a walking, talking pet goldfish. Not very valuable but handy to keep in a small bowl until you – or your soul – dies. Then away down the toilet you go, and no looking back.

Best strategy?

Decide that unless the request, aka demand, fits seamlessly with your plans, don't do it. Even if you fancy doing whatever is being demanded, just don't do it. Once in a very rare while you will be cutting your nose off to spite your face, but live with it. You need to stand up for yourself and cut those strings and that means for every time they are tugged.

Does your parent blame or attack you?

Another 'hell, yeah', sadly. As far as the toxic parent is concerned, you are on earth for one main reason, and that is to take the flak for everything that happens to them or, possibly, your golden child sibling(s). Sharing experiences about this always tends to sound a bit shouty and 'he said, she said' and that is part of the problem. This will begin when you are very little and so it is unlikely that you will even be aware for much of your young life that this is abnormal. Some of the toxic behaviours in the list don't kick in until you are older and beginning to break away, so the control is ramped up. But blame is something that even a baby can get – kept them up all night, cost them too much money for the pram, ruined their career trajectory etc – because clearly, it was that baby's choice to be born and therefore to blame for the lot.

As I mentioned before, I was illegitimate, and while that means pretty much nothing now – in 2021, for example more babies (51%) were born to unmarried mothers in England and Wales than to those in a marriage or civil partnership for the first time since records began in 1845 – to her it was a big deal. Actually, a bigger deal than it need have been as by the time I was born, it was becoming less of a stigma. She didn't really let it make much of a crimp in her life. We lived with my grandparents and they pretty much brought me up. I didn't move in with her and my stepdad (who married her when I was almost four years old) until I was seven and then all I did was sleep at their house, eating all my meals with my grandparents. It did mess up my nana's life though – she had just got herself her first job outside helping on the smallholding for the best part of thirty years – as she was back in a childcare role. She didn't mind, I don't think – she and my grandfather loved me unconditionally for the rest of their lives. So, I was luckier there than many children of toxic parents – a bright spot in the gloom.

It was therefore my fault that I was born. I have never really managed to work out the logic of that, but what toxic parent has ever used logic? My soldier birth father was a non-commissioned officer and was away when I was born until I was around nine months old. She went, with other wives and girlfriends I assume, to welcome the regiment back to barracks, with me, cute as a bug, in her arms.

Not cute enough, though, because turns out he has a wife somewhere else and so no amount of babies, no matter how cute, were going to get her the cottage with roses round the door and the classic happy ending complete with bluebirds. My fault, clearly.

I never got credit, by the way, for the fact that everyone says that my stepdad (as explained before, my dad in every respect but birth) married her as much to get me as a daughter as her as a wife. And why not – did I say I was cute as a bug? Time moves on and their own baby is born, a little boy who as far as I know began his life healthy and normal. He was damaged, as the family narrative goes, by a vaccine (not the safe option then that it is now) although this was never discussed for the rest of his life and indeed, his clear learning problems were never addressed either, leaving him disadvantaged in a totally unnecessary way. Although even she didn't have the brass faced cheek to blame me for his issues, it *was* my fault that I could do more than he could, that I was clearly bright and academic. Or, in toxic parent speak, showing off.

I have already addressed the 'working fingers to the bone' issue, and of course that never really ends. Once they have stopped actually doing that (if it ever really happened at all) the toxic parent will bemoan the fact that because of you and the need to WTFTTB, they are in shocking health and so therefore, this is all your fault. I made things worse by not inheriting the family rheumatism (auto-immune problems which beset that bloodline) and so somehow, by not having knotted fingers and dodgy hips, I am mocking those who do. And this is the thing with blame – anything can be turned to the big purpose

When things get physical

I have chosen to take 'attack' literally here, although I don't think that was the intention of the list compilers. Not all toxic parents are physically violent and I think that that is an essential point to make. They prefer to vent their toxicity in being horrible human beings, belittling, lying, all the fun stuff. Just a small proportion of them actually physically hurt their children and of course, it is of fairly short duration (as a rule – hands up who remembers the skillet scene in *Throw Momma from the Train*) because even kids of toxic parents grow too big to hit in the end. Because I lived largely with my grandparents until I was six or seven years old, I suppose that puts the timescale of the violence as about ten years of my life but I think most people would agree that that is ten years too long.

I don't intend to make a list here of the physical abuse I suffered but its main component was that it would come out of the blue. It wasn't generally linked to any one event, but could come hours or days after the trigger. So, to give one example, I was on holiday from school (my school wasn't always off when the others were) and was taking some much needed time with no one else in the house to catch up on some reading – *Wuthering Heights*, as memory serves. My mother came in (from WHFTTB I expect) and called something indistinct. I assumed it was a greeting (fat chance) but it turns out, it was a command to get the kettle on and generally make myself useful. I didn't.

Slow forward about four hours and by then I had stopped reading and was putting my coat on to go up to my grandparents' house for a natter and my tea, as was the usual thing. As I was going out of the house, I was suddenly pulled back with an agonising pain in my head. As I had gone through the hall, she had hurtled out of the kitchen, wailing like a banshee and wound one of my long curls round a couple of her fingers. She yanked on it so hard most of the hair came out and – and I don't know where I got the strength from – I kept on walking, leaving her with the hair in her hand. I was getting on at this point, probably about fifteen, and she didn't hit me or hurt me much after that, I was too big. But before that, we had the broom, the hot iron already mentioned, the spade ... anything in hand, because she never planned the outbursts, I don't think. Thank goodness she didn't use a carving knife (her cooking was more of the fry until it dies kind) or I might be a statistic of a different kind.

More subtle abuse was basic ill treatment and withdrawal of what she would call 'privileges' and most people would call 'normal life'; baths, sanitary products, hairbrush, pens, ink, books. Just as a tweakment of general abuse, she would also give my possessions away, the book from the bedside table, clothes, ornaments and gifts, the theory being, I guess, that as a cypher, I didn't need the things that other people did.

So, a slightly niche type of toxicity, but damaging for all that.

DOES YOUR PARENT TAKE RESPONSIBILITY AND APOLOGIZE?

I can honestly say, hand on heart, that I never, ever heard my mother say the word 'sorry'. To anyone, that is. I think that this is perhaps *the* section of toxicity which is most likely to bleed across into everyday life. Nothing has ever, *ever* been my mother's fault. Not ever. She has had – because of her behaviour – many issues both at work and with neighbours (I won't say friends, because she has had precious few of those, mainly just acquaintances) just because she will never assume the responsibility of agreeing that it was her fault. This can make things very difficult for the child of a toxic parent as they get older and get more involved with interactions with, say, councils, public bodies of all kinds like hospitals, care givers. One essential thing to remind yourself of, though, is that you will have had plenty of practice over the years at appeasement. Of wronged people, often strangers, who when they get no redress from the toxic one, turn on (it would be nice if it was 'to' but no, usually it is 'on') you. I have many examples of this, but two stand out.

When our first child was small, my mother came to stay. Not to help, you understand. Just stay. Fortunately, we had an angel baby and so it wasn't too bad. Anyway, one morning we thought we would take her to our favourite coffee shop and walking there from the car park, we see an old lady who has to be described as a character – strange clothes, absolutely stonkingly enormous standard poodle and a load of bags – across the road. To be fair, she was an arresting sight and mother wasn't used to her but even so, it was not cool to shriek (yes, and point) 'Look at 'er! Look! Look!' as if she were just a hologram or a piece of street art.

At this point, the old dear has crossed to our side and very politely, in her usual cut glass tones, says, 'Can I help you?'

Mother looks startled and then at my husband and me but says nothing.

'I'm asking *you*, my dear,' says the old lady. 'Can I help you with something?'

No reply from mother and the usual tugging of our clothing to get us away from a situation she can't handle. No farting, as I recall. But then, having just about got away with some dignity intact, she starts yelling about the woman *again*. At this point, we forget the coffee and just go home because ... basically, because we both wanted to just dig a hole and jump into it. At home, no apology, no 'I'm sorry I made things awkward for you' – just nothing. Just repetitions without number of what a strange woman that was. En't she? En't she? Strange?

The other story is more serious. We rationed time with her for our kids because, well, we are quite fond of them and didn't want any of them to be poisoned (food allergies are for sissies) or other such disasters. One summer, though, we let her have one for a week. They didn't last a week, being brought home early by my dad and their lodger (see later) because they really could see this wasn't working out. However, before their intervention, they went to a theme park. Gulliver's World of Adventures, as memory serves. Anyway, along with all toxic parents, my mother never bothered to pre-plan because the world will budge aside for her, of course, so planning is for other people.

However, once inside the park, she was way out of her comfort zone. She didn't understand the queuing system, how to tell if your kid is the right size for a ride etc and so it looked as if it was going to be a pretty boring visit, just standing inside the entranceway, looking on. But wait! She has an idea. A family with a child about the age of ours came past and she turned to them and ... I sweat just writing this down ... asked them if our darling child could go round the park with them? They said yes, more in amazement than anything I suspect and so they arranged to meet in the café in such and such a time and that was it. No 'what is your name?' 'Where is your car?' 'Where are you from?' Just – here's the kid, here's a fiver for treats ... (I nearly said 'thank you' but there is no way she would have said that). Happily, as you may have guessed, it was all okay but ... honestly? People actually do that? With someone else's child? And of course, there is the thing. He wasn't someone else's child. Because he was *her* child. And just as worthless as his actual mother, to her.

I said two stories, but I can't leave this one out. This was not a food allergy situation, because my dad was always tough on that, even though it went against his nature. It was an extreme dislike, sweetcorn, as it happens. On a rare visit, they took one of the kids out for lunch – different kid, we are equal opportunities parents when it comes to putting them at risk of death by grandmother. He hated sweetcorn, just hated it, the texture, the smell, the lot. So, they went out for lunch and there, looming on his plate, was a pile of sweetcorn. Which, of course, she forced him to eat. And which, of course, he threw up all over the table. When they got home he was still really distressed but did she say sorry? Of course not. Because it was his fault, for gobbling his food. There was no way he would gobble sweetcorn, or even be in the room with it, for preference. But still – his fault. And the fact that he had an eating disorder from that moment for another six years –

clearly not her fault either, if she was any judge.

So, long stories short – never, *ever* expect your toxic parent to take responsibility for their actions. Because they literally never, *ever* will.

DOES YOUR PARENT RESPECT YOUR PHYSICAL AND EMOTIONAL BOUNDARIES?

Boundaries? What are they? My mother was that strange amalgam of a person pathologically averse to nudity and references to sex whilst also being prone to bursting into rooms unannounced. Let's face it, that combo is never going to end well. I don't think I ever heard her say the words sex, pregnant or love out loud. Instead, she would do some kind of borderline insane pantomime or just mouth them very deliberately. Remember Les Dawson and Roy Barraclough? Like that. Only not funny.

Physical boundaries are only part of it, of course. Because the boundaries as to when to tell a 'story' and when not to are even more important, if that is possible. Add in the fact that it is less than 50% likely that the story is even true and it all becomes more toe-curling still. There are so many stories of boundary crossing when I was a child that I struggle to choose just one. She would tell anyone who would listen that ... spoiler alert, somewhat scatological tale coming up ... that my shit smelled worse than anything she had ever smelled before. I doubt that is true, but it was a story told well into my teens, including one occasion that still makes me squirm, to a boyfriend as we left to go on our first date. Two things to take away from that – where was the visit to the doctor? And isn't it the food I was being given that would cause that – not that she actually fed me much, that was down to my grandparents until I left home. I was also constantly the butt of her oversharing about blowing my nose (too loud, apparently) and puberty being delayed – not put that way and also (no surprise) not actually true.

Once I got married, the tales began to become even more wild and inappropriate. We were 'having trouble' (actually, no, but you knew that) and then once that story wouldn't fly any more, the 'babby ent normal'. Why anyone would want to share that, even if true, I have no idea. And of course, it wasn't – there was no way on God's green earth I would ever have shared any medical news at all. Once there was a grandchild, oh, heavens above, what rich pickings for the tellings of tall tales. Not one of the below is true.

I would like to express this in her odd patois, used, as far as I can tell, only when I was present. I have checked with people, linguists, neurosurgeons, educationalists and a whole slew of geriatricians and have no answer still. But I won't because it is really, really irritating for anything more than a line or so.

The story goes like this. Once, we were on a train. This falls at the first as I have no memory of ever catching a train with her. My son was around three and suddenly, in front of a rather startled elderly gentleman sitting opposite, he yanked up my blouse and cupped my boobs and said loudly, 'These are mine, these are.' I'll let you take that in for a bit. Okay, feeling better now?

The old gent, apparently, smiled and said, 'Are they now?' and went back to his newspaper. I sat there smiling smugly as junior bounced my tits around and then, tiring of his sport, sat down.

Writing this down for the first time, I can't work out why, when she said it first – and she said it literally dozens of times over the years – I didn't say 'How bloody ridiculous' and forbid her to tell such a load of arrant tosh again. But I didn't. Because, and this is the problem with all toxic parents, when they are embarked on a cute little tits-on-a-train story, you let them tell it, because it is less embarrassing than many other personal stories they feel it is their right to share. Enabling. That, sadly, is the name of the game.

Oversharing is a terrible invasion of the other person's privacy. Whether your poo smells or not (and let's face it, everyone's does) is not something that needs to be discussed in a bus queue. Made up stories about ... not sure. Was it the precocity of my child, the way I was parenting, the propensity for old chaps to be embarrassed? Made up is the main text here, because if you want to tell a funny story – assuming that it is, indeed, funny – then just do it. But don't make it sound like the gospel truth when it brings someone else down.

Physical boundaries were not really a problem, as she preferred not to touch me. Ever. Even making desperately slow progress in hospital or out shopping, she would rather do it without my arm. She couldn't keep her hands off my husband, though, and latterly told everyone that he had been her boyfriend first, and I stole him. Quite a nifty trick, but it became, in her dementia, a real thing. But even before that, she would offer to take off her top so he could borrow it to keep warm, would generally squeeze and manhandle him at any opportunity. If I were to kiss him, though – we are fans of PDAs – she would shout 'Stop mauling him about'; and mean it. So, I suppose she was invading a physical boundary, the one that encircled me and my other half.

What to do if this happens to you

It is really important to nip this in the bud as soon as possible. If you are a family member of a child or young adult whose boundaries are being invaded, take all steps you can to prevent it. It is a hidden issue in many families, but if children flinch or move away when a parent or carer comes near, watch carefully. If a parent is over-sharing personal details, then stop them at the get go. Don't let the story become family currency, because, believe me, it isn't at all amusing and can end up causing all kinds of problems along the way. It was years, for example, before I would use the loo outside the home, in case I smelled. It gave me serious bowel issues that took me some twenty years to overcome – 'funny' story at one level, danger to health at the other.

DOES YOUR PARENT DISREGARD YOUR FEELINGS AND NEEDS?

This is another of those tricky ones because the toxic parent isn't disregarding your feelings or needs, they simply don't consider that you have either. This is actually another place in which you are sharing the situation with the rest of the world. No matter what is happening, your toxic parent will be the only one who can win. Whether it is a choice of where to go to eat, shop, holiday or what colour to paint the bathroom, it is their way or the highway. The blame here probably lies in generations now gone, parents or grandparents who allowed the coercion to embed itself in your parent's psyche to the extent that now, they hardly know they are doing it.

My mother never had a job with much hierarchy involved in it, it was mainly just her and her colleagues and one boss overall. Despite that, she managed to align herself with that boss, to the extent that many people who just popped in (delivery drivers etc) assumed she was his wife. This wasn't just one job, it was throughout about a thirty year period, with the age gap between the boss and her getting so wide in the end that the scam didn't work any more. In only a few cases was she dispensed with, because she lived in a small place and everyone knew everyone else, so things could get a bit gnarly. But on the occasions when she was 'let go', she managed to weep and wail to such an extent that the whole neighbourhood was divided, mostly on her side. And in a way, you had to almost feel sorry for her because I genuinely believe she couldn't see what she had done wrong, demeaning other staff, alienating clients, making a thirty-year-old cringe with embarrassment when as a seventy-year-old she tried to pass as his wife.

So this is one that I don't think needs a tick on your list. If your mother is toxic, this is a given. But it won't be just aimed at you. It is her world view and so everyone within a million miles is going to get exactly the same. I have seen the blank expression come over her face when someone says she has hurt so and so's feelings. Because, to her, that is clearly impossible, as they have none. Not as important as hers, anyway.

In this, she was in a weird folie a deux with her brother. If anything went wrong in her life, he would spring into attack mode. It just so happens that my mother was not 100% honest, which is nothing to do with general toxicity and everything to do with having an eye to the main chance. Nothing big, but if money was in her hands which didn't belong to her, let's just say that not all of it would make it home. On one occasion, she had run a local event for a while and then gave it up. After a year or two, someone wanted to restart it and asked her for the books. The money this thing made was not big but suffice to say, it was no longer around and no books had been kept. This was a problem as there was a constitution to consider and so it all got a bit shouty. So uncle took it upon himself to go round the village bad-mouthing the well-meaning person who had unwittingly got in the middle of this, accusing him of all kinds of dreadful things. They thought that that was alright, to smear someone who had done no wrong, to save their own faces.

And you, as the child of a toxic parent, will recognise this as a daily occurrence, no doubt. You just didn't know they were hurting your feelings, because for years, you didn't know you had any.

Fallout

Because this behaviour is a little more nebulous than some and is a little like trying to prove a negative, the fallout on a child can be severe. You can grow up seeing slights everywhere, as your parent does, while not understanding that respect goes both ways. This can have a huge effect on childhood friendships and later work connections. Hopefully, you will find a partner nice enough to work things through with you, but if not, you could end up in a repeat of your home situation, where your feelings are not respected and you in return respect no one. Probably nobody will ever put a label on this and you may well end up quite lonely, through no fault of your own. It is important to look carefully at the situation if ever you take offence and think through whether perhaps you had shown less than appropriate care when dealing with the feelings of someone else.

Alex Farrell

DOES YOUR PARENT ENVY OR COMPETE WITH YOU?

When I first saw this on a list to check if your parent was toxic, I literally whooped for joy. This is not one which is on every list and yet when it crops up, I would imagine it gets more ticks than any other single category. The toxic parent *lives* to compete and it is probably the saddest category of all. Because why would a grown woman want to 'beat' a small child in anything? Haven't they had their own chance of ... oh, I dunno, choose your own thing here. Let's pick the 'Best Saucer Garden for the Under-Fives' at the flower show. There isn't an adult version of this, so the toxic parent is a bit stuck. In this respect it is like the dancing class's *Swan Lake* attempt or the Recorder Class at the music festival. They can't compete directly, so they sabotage.

Sabotage Stage 1

You come home from school or wherever, excited to have been cast as the third sheep or whatever role you have snagged. If you have a solo or a starring part, prepare for the sabotage to be more complex but Stage 1 is essentially a never ending take down. When your dad gets home, a friend pops in, your toxic mother will pull you out of whatever you are doing and demand that you tell the newly arrived person your news. She will position herself slightly behind you, so that as you make the announcement, she can roll her eyes and generally gurn so the person knows that this role is nothing. She will then cap your story with when she was second sheep, had a much longer/more difficult solo when she was years younger. So already, you can feel the gilt peeling off your gingerbread.

Sabotage Stage 2

You need to practice. Tough luck. As in previous categories, you will be ruining her life. How can she rest after WHFTTB with that racket going on. The racket can be as little as turning a page, but still. When *she* was first sheep, she never made a sound or indeed needed any preparation, because such things have always come naturally to her.

Sabotage Stage 3

You need a costume. Also tough luck. She will make one, but it won't be the same as the others (in the case of the sheep) or to specs (anything else). If it is needed by Tuesday morning, it will be ready Tuesday afternoon. When she was the shepherd, she made her own costume. Oh – you're only five? Well, it's time you learned.

Performance Day

Someone made your costume for you, you look like all the other sheep, you have had tucks taken in the back of your enormous dress/gussets let into your unfeasibly tight dress and you are facing your public. You scan the audience for the toxic one. Yup, she's there, but she isn't looking at you, she is scrolling on her phone. When the headmistress or whoever is MC asks for phones to be silenced or preferably switched off, she sighs audibly and stands so as to stash it away. She says loudly to her probably somewhat startled neighbour that when she played the part of the owner of every sheep on the planet, no one would have noticed a ringing phone, so immersive was her performance. You do your thing, baaing, hitting A above top C, whatever it might be. You glance across. She is bent down, doing something to her shoelace.

At home

Your performance will never, *ever* be mentioned again. Unless you screwed up somehow, in which case she will never leave it alone. In her role as creator of all sheep in the Universe, she was perfect, she did not put a foot wrong, whereas you ... [eye roll] ... she will never be able to look the neighbours in the eye again.

Competition will cover any aspect of your life, even ones where she can't possibly compete with you. If your chosen career takes you to unprecedented heights, no matter. So, she is not the Director General of the UN, but she has better teeth than you, and at the end of the day, that is all that matters.

But surely, we all compete, don't we?

It is true that without a bit of healthy competition, the world would now consist of about twelve people lying on sofas going 'Whatev*ah*' but that is healthy competition. Unhealthy competition is wanting to beat your child at everything, from Ludo up. This specific example didn't apply to my mother, but a friend of mine at work, while pregnant with her first child, had the unsettling news that her mother had sold her house to pay for IVF and was now also pregnant. Now *that's* competitive! You don't have to go that far to be in an unhealthy competition. We always taught our children that, once they were able to work games out themselves, we would not be 'cheating' in order to let them win and I have to say that the day I can beat any of them at Scrabble will be the day hell freezes over. When a parent cheats to win because they can't bear to lose, that's when you really are at the mercy of a crazy person – and yet many of us put up with that for decades. The trick is to learn when competition stops and coercion and bullying begin.

The green-eyed monster

Jealousy is a terrible thing and we have all known people who suffer from it. One friend we had was always terribly jealous, sometimes of the least thing, and would become very rude and abrasive and even destructive when she was in its grip. We stood it for years until it became too much and the day we parted company was a real relief, even though we felt bad for leaving her husband just that bit more alone. Everyone has a story like that. But what everyone would agree on would be that no parent should ever be jealous of their child. Because, surely, their child is great at what they do, or has achieved a degree of life success in the way of house, car, etc, only because of their fabulous upbringing. So, a parent is proud of their child, right?

Wrong.

The toxic parent wants to actually *be* their child, but a better version. They will hijack their achievements and deny that the child did it – in my mother's case, pieces of artwork and also cooking (which she couldn't do and I can) – and will even hijack friends, which is odd, because by definition there is a generation between them. My mother took it to absurd lengths, being so jealous of me that she would claim that my husband loved her really and only married me on the rebound. Trying to pick the logic out of that one could drive you literally crazy if you're not careful.

It is sometimes hard to tell jealousy from general putting down. One of my mother's classics when leaving one of our children's new house (three bed, two bath, two recep on a nice street, not too shabby!) was to shrug – having refused to sit down and have a cup of tea – on the step, look it up and down disparagingly and say ''S'allri for them as wants it.' You can tell how pissed off and eaten up with jealousy she was – she used the 'useless daughter' patois on a more remote family member.

You can't fix a jealous toxic parent. It is bred in their bones and all you can do is look on in amazement as they eat themselves from the inside.

DOES YOUR PARENT TREAT ALL THEIR CHILDREN THE SAME?

This is one which will very much depend on the family makeup, of course. I had one brother, who had lots of health and developmental issues, so I don't think that my experience is the norm by any means. Even so, I was the 'scapegoat child' which is what I hear from many other people with toxic parents. Whatever you do if this applies to you, it will never be right. You will always be uglier, stupider, fatter, slower, more annoying, less grateful and all round just not as wonderful as your siblings. This can be stretched to cousins as well if required and never mind if the cousins and their parents are mocked and derided out of their earshot. When they are present, you will always be the worst person in the room.

It is hard for the sibling in this situation too, I think. A sensitive one will know that there is something not right, but as the one being given the present they asked for, the food they prefer, the little perks of childhood that make the world go round – and I am just thinking a kind word or a kiss here, not diamonds – they don't feel they can complain. There is always the risk that if they do, then they will be in the doghouse as well, which isn't something anyone would choose, especially a child. Unfortunately, as people get older, this sense of entitlement, of being the golden child, is something which beds in and their gift from their devoted parent is that they almost always grow up to be utter dicks. I can't help feeling that that is Karma in action.

This is a short section because of my lack of first-hand knowledge, but I think that, by and large, a toxic parent is a toxic parent and if they are nice to your sister or brother, then you should feel sorry for them. You have learned how to be a nice person despite it all. They, to pinch a social media acronym for now, ATAH.

BONUS CHAPTER
WHEN THEY ARE FINALLY
DEAD

I had to wait an unconscionable time for this but it will finally happen, I promise. What will happen then will depend on your family and your friends as to whether they understand why you are turning cartwheels all around the garden. I am lucky enough to have a clutch of fabulous friends who understand and some family, but in the main, this is the conversation you can expect to have:

You: My mother died last week.
Them: Oh, I am so sorry.
You: Thank you, but you needn't be. She was, as you must remember from other conversations where I have literally wept on your shoulder, an evil, manipulative, grasping, lying tyrant. The world is better off.
Them: But she is your mother, after all.
You: Not really. After not a kind word all my life, I don't think she qualifies.
Them: But she is your mother, though. You must have loved her.
You: Nope.
Them: But she *is* your mother.

You: I don't think we are going to agree on this. So ... can we just leave it, please?

And so, you leave it. And two things happen. They go away and think about it and finally twig that just by an accident of birth, you were that person's offspring. Not child. Not daughter or son. Not beloved. Not even liked. You were just a collection of cells that they contributed to. They didn't love you, so why are you being forced to love them? That person will then hopefully send you a message of support or, if near enough, give you a hug strong enough to potentially break a rib.

The second thing will be that that person will go home and mull it over and discover that their decision on this is ... she is your mother, after all. That person probably has no place in your life. They have the potential to become as toxic as your parent, because they can't see that anyone else is allowed to be right whilst not following the path that they set them to follow.

In the weeks that have passed since my mother died, I have had many different reactions, some so upsetting that I don't think I will ever recover from the bile and spite. I think the thing that strikes me there is that, well, she is my mother after all and she is dead so ... where is their sympathy for me, the poor bereaved child? Apparently nowhere, because I am that strange chimera, the sadly orphaned and the devil incarnate. You don't see that many of those about, do you? As the child of a toxic parent, this is the Scylla and Charybdis you will have to negotiate. You will need to decide whether to be a total hypocrite and pretend you are distraught but not make too many enemies or you will be honest and have at least half the world hate you.

I chose honesty. I have lived my whole life under the cloud of someone so innately dishonest that she stole from charities, lied about people when they were scarcely out of the door and then fawned on them next time they met, encouraged her son to commit benefits fraud. Of someone who could throw tantrums in her sixties that would put a toddler to shame, literally, on one occasion, clawing at me and trying to pull me off a stepladder because she didn't want me to set up digital tv (when the whole country's coverage of analogue was about to be shut down). Of someone who thought nothing of writing to my about to be employers (straight out of school) telling them I was 'unbalanced' because she didn't want me to move to London. Of someone who ... but let's face it, no book is long enough to list everything. The time she took my lightbulbs out of my trusty Raleigh Wisp so I had to push it home six miles in the dark. The refusal to let me use deodorant or bathe. To have toothpaste. Buying all my clothes just that threat too small, so I could be called fat with what she considered justification.

My honesty, in conversation with the people who remind me that she is my mother after all, does not go into the details. I don't want the tuts, the shakes of the head, the information that she was lovely, generous, so kind to everyone. No, everyone, she was not. You didn't hear her laughing like something from the opening scenes of *Macbeth* as soon as you had left the building. How your hair was like straw, your brain was like a pea, your husband was knocking off the neighbour. How we laughed! Or she did, at least. Did it occur to you to wonder why there were no books to be scrutinized when she collected money for charity? Did you not wonder why she didn't let anyone help? I don't suppose you stopped to wonder why her daughter never joined in with any swimming, athletics or anything else requiring bare limbs – bruises are embarrassing to the recipients, never the givers.

So, no details. Just a small tight smile when people say they are sorry. If they want to be sorry, that is their option, of course.

But I am not sorry.

And I hope that this book has given you the permission you need to feel that you don't need to be sorry either.

If you need support:
If you are under 18, Childline is a good start. 0800 1111 – totally confidential – is the number to ring and sometimes, just a chat with someone understanding will put you on the path to coping. If physical abuse, coercion or bullying is involved – which it will be – then they are all criminal offences and will be dealt with accordingly.

Samaritans are fabulous and a listening ear at all times. 116 123 is the number and it is free from all phones. Breaking silence is the big thing with anything as apparently 'secret' as having a toxic parent, and they are trained to listen, so you are with a safe pair of ears when you ring them. Also totally confidential, of course.

Therapy is a way forward and for me was a way of learning to talk about things. Your GP can recommend someone or you can look online. You might not be as lucky as I was and it may take you a time or two to find The One, but if it helps you to get things into perspective and start making a difference to your life by stepping away or whatever is needed, then it is worth the journey.

But mainly, my advice – and I am not a therapist or anything official, just a fellow traveller – is to keep your honesty and integrity, don't feel it is your responsibility that you have a toxic parent. Don't let the pattern repeat itself. Support anyone who you find through conversations are suffering too. And finally, remember Julian of Norwich, my go-to-woman when things are bad.

All shall be well
And all shall be well
And all manner of things shall be well.

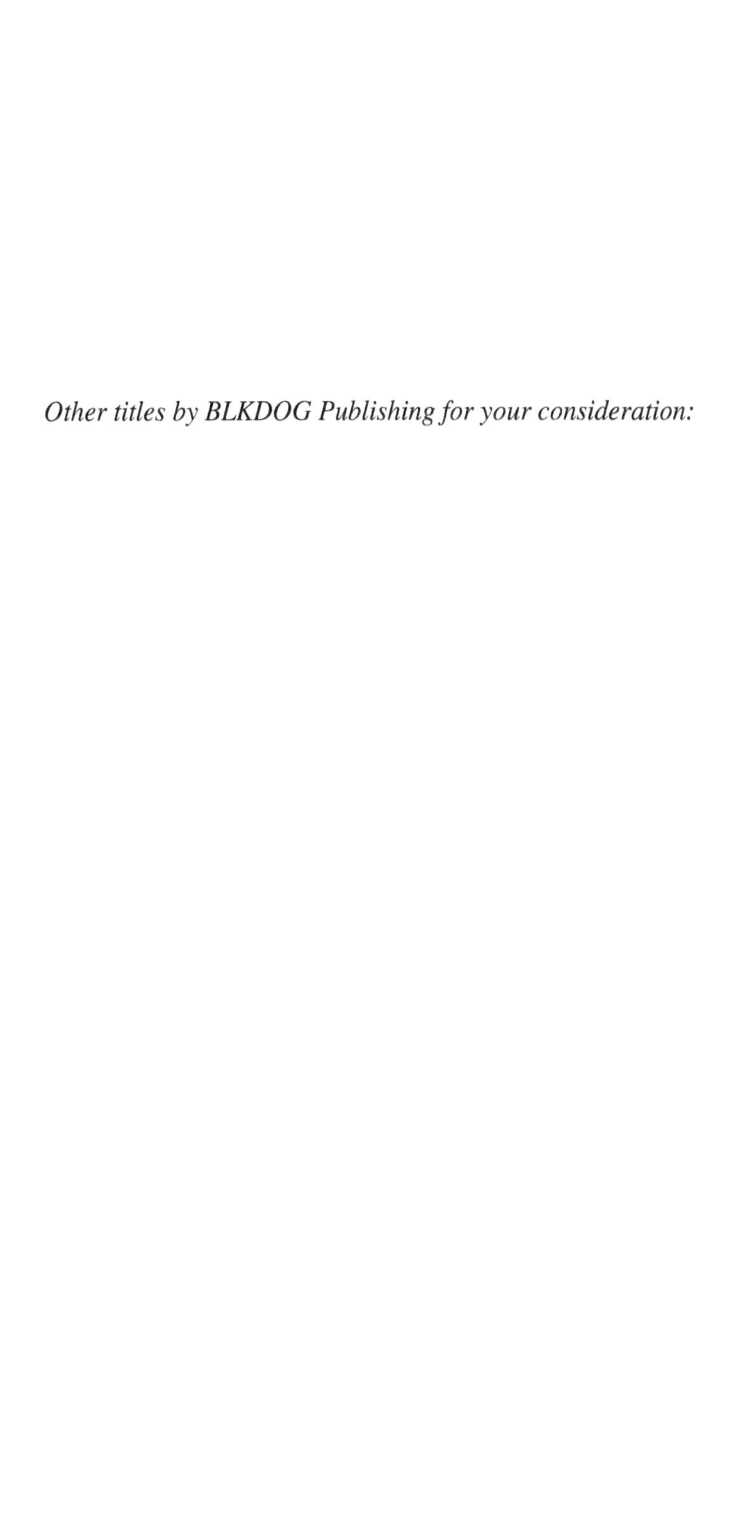

Other titles by BLKDOG Publishing for your consideration:

Britannia: The Wall
By Richard Denham & M. J. Trow

THE END OF ROMAN BRITAIN BEGINS.

The story opens in 367 AD. Four soldiers - Justinus, Paternus, Leocadius and Vitalis - are out hunting for food supplies at an outpost of Hadrian's Wall, when the Wall comes under attack.

The four find their fort destroyed, their comrades killed, and Paternus is unable to find his wife and son. As they run south to Eboracum, they realize that this is no ordinary border raid. Ranged against the Romans at the edge of the world are four different peoples, and they have banded together under a mysterious leader who wears a silver mask and uses the name Valentinus - man of Valentia, the turbulent area north of the Wall.

Faced with questions they are hard-pressed to answer, Leocadius blurts out a story that makes the men Heroes of the Wall. Their lives change not only when Valentinus begins his lethal sweep across Britannia but as soon as Leo's lie is out in the world, growing and changing as it goes.

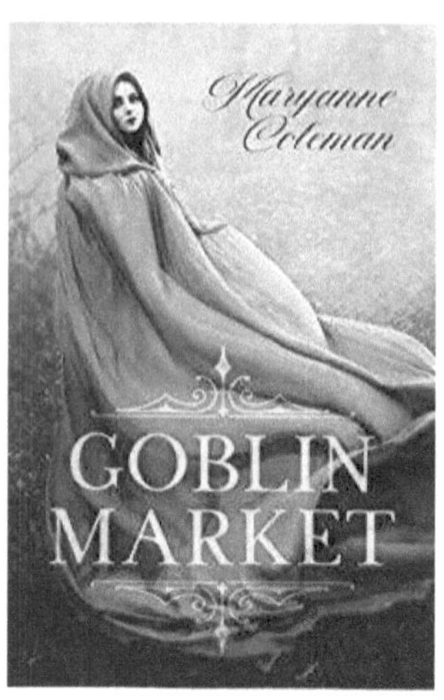

Goblin Market
By Maryanne Coleman

Have you ever wondered what happened to the faeries you used to believe in? They lived at the bottom of the garden and left rings in the grass and sparkling glamour in the air to remind you where they were. But that was then – now you might find them in places you might not think to look. They might be stacking shelves, delivering milk or weighing babies at the clinic. Open your eyes and keep your wits about you and you might see them.

But no one is looking any more and that is hard for a Faerie Queen to bear and Titania has had enough. When Titania stamps her foot, everyone in Faerieland jumps; publicity is what they need. Television, magazines. But that sort of thing is much more the remit of the bad boys of the Unseelie Court, the ones who weave a new kind of magic; the World Wide Web. Here is Puck re-learning how to fly; Leanne the agent who really is a vampire; Oberon's Boys playing cards behind the wainscoting; Black Annis, the bag-lady from Hainault, all gathered in a Restoration comedy that is strictly twenty-first century.

Fade
By Bethan White

There is nothing extraordinary about Chris Rowan. Each day he wakes to the same faces, has the same breakfast, the same commute, the same sort of homes he tries to rent out to unsuspecting tenants.

There is nothing extraordinary about Chris Rowan. That is apart from the black dog that haunts his nightmares and an unexpected encounter with a long forgotten demon from his past. A nudge that will send Chris on his own downward spiral, from which there may be no escape.

There is nothing extraordinary about Chris Rowan...

www.blkdogpublishing.com

www.ingramcontent.com/pod-product-compliance
Lightning Source LLC
Chambersburg PA
CBHW051758130726
47987CB00003B/1018